I0419722

Body Language 101

*What A Person's Body Language Is Really Telling You…
And How You Can Use It To Your Advantage*

By Michele Gilbert

<u>Visit My Amazon Author Page</u>

Table of contents

Introduction

Talk to the Hand

Weapons of Mass Induction

Look Into My Eyes

The Voice of Reason

Stand Up Straight

Habitual Habits

In Perfect Harmony

Your Library

Conclusion

Introduction

I want to thank you and congratulate you for downloading the book, *Body Language 101*

This book contains proven steps and strategies on how to understand body language.

Are you tired of watching amazing detectives on the television figuring out everything that you're missing in the real world? Do you feel like you're missing half of what is being said to you when you're not really picking up the right signals? Well, there's a good chance that you're missing all of the nonverbal signals that are being sent your way.

Well, no more! From this day forward, you're going to be the man that picks up on all the subtle signs, all the secret hints, and all the missing broadcasts that the people around you are sending. You're going to be able to turn the most silent, uptight person you know into an open book. But only if you start by reading this book. So what are you waiting for?

Thanks again for downloading this book, I hope you enjoy it!

Dedicated to those who choose to stretch beyond their own limits and to seek a more abundant and fulfilling life.

Your thoughts are creative.

Michele Gilbert

Talk to the Hand

I don't know about you, but when I watch shows like L☐☐ ☐e or ☐☐☐☐☐☐ so often, I really, really wish that I could be that good. Heck, after I watched ☐☐ ☐en☐☐☐for the first time, I was studying everyone. I stared at footprints trying to see if I could tell whether the person walking was right handed or left handed. Not only is this super impractical for me as an actual skill, but its super addicting. The thing is, it's all about studying people and watching them, but there's a science to it. I may not be out there catching criminals red handed for having a nervous tell, but it has helped me read situations and understand things that I previously missed.

So sure, you might not catch your arch-nemesis, but you might be able to understand things a little better with a little study of body language. And that's why I'm here. Body language is not just for detectives out there looking to catch murderers and thieves. Body language is the key to understanding the unspoken words that our body is communicating so heavily without our knowledge. Not only will this help you understand and relate to people better, but it'll make it so that you are aware of your own presence to others.

Nonverbal communication makes up the majority of our communication and most of us are clueless to the actual comprehension and understanding of it. That means that those who do not invest time in learning what to say in our nonverbal appearance are missing so much. But the truth is, we don't miss all of it. We have come to silently absorb and understand nonverbal communication, regardless of whether we know it or not. It's the art of learning to understand something we already know and to heighten our understanding and acceptance of what's being communicated to us. It's tricky, I know, but it's not impossible to understand.

What I'm going to tell you in this book is going to make sense to you and a lot of it is going to feel familiar, like you already knew that. Well, the reason for that is that you you've been picking up these silent transmissions for years, you just haven't acknowledged them or put a name to some of the habits you've already taught yourself.

So stick around and start to see if you can't agree or relate to some of the information you're going to receive. But more importantly, I want to address your homework before we start getting into the gritty, deep stuff. For instance, I want you to start watching people around you.

Observation is the birth of understanding and without a true sense of observance or a keen eye for noticing the little things, you're not going to pick up on some of these traits. When someone is talking to you, you're going to need to start watching them. Notice how they're standing, note the posture, have you looked at their eyes, what about the overall harmony of their face, and what are they doing with their hands? All of these things need to be running through your mind to really catch what is being conveyed to you. But not just watching their body, note the tones they're using, and the words that they're selecting. These are all going to tell you what sort of body language comes with certain attitudes and emotions. It all ties together and it is all relevant when it comes to understanding body language. So start opening your eyes and let's have a look at what they're trying to say to you.

Are you ready?

Weapons of Mass Induction

Though Sherlock Holmes often touts his use of deductive reasoning, it is actually the opposite that we're going to focus on with you, because right now, you're a student. For those of you that do not know, inductive reasoning starts with observations that slowly build a pattern that you will then form into a hypothesis until it is proven right or wrong. If you're right, then you have a theory.

For example, Kayla touches her hair a lot when she talks to Hot Mike, but not when she's talking to anyone else. So, every time I see Kayla talking to Hot Mike and she's touching her hair, that might be a cue that she likes Hot Mike. So, until I'm proven wrong, I'm certain that I have a theory that when a woman likes a man, she'll touch her hair unconsciously.

Viola, you have just jumped from observation to theory until proven wrong. Of course, when you're Sherlock Holmes level, you'll be using the art of deductive reasoning which starts at a theory and then tested with a hypothesis and observations until you have a conclusion. I think it's time for another example to prove this one to you.

Okay, so Angry Pete is a born liar and is known for lying, so you're going to deduce a trait from pathological liars. So, you're going to ask Angry Pete if he took your lunch, because you're fairly certain that he did. You think that when Pete is telling you a lie, he's going to try his hardest to maintain eye contact because he wants to make sure you're buying his lie and he'll know you'll suspect him of lying if he glances away. So, you approach Angry Pete and ask him if he ate you bologna and mustard sandwich. He tells you no while keeping strict eye contact and gives you an implausible story, all the while having mustard on his lips. Therefore, you conclude that not only did Angry Pete eat your sandwich, but that pathological liars maintain eye contact religiously when telling you a lie.

You have just performed deductive reasoning and an experiment to find the truth. These are going to be crucial in your learning beyond this book and they are tools that you should begin to master as soon as possible. Not only are they a great life skill, but you're going to be able to push your learning beyond this book with them.

Now, why is it important to know these things? Well, the answer is that behavioral studies and body language experts are all going to tell you that coming to understand body language is all about trial and error, which means they're using inductive and deductive reasoning until they're proven wrong. Note right now that there are exceptions to everything that I'm going to be telling you. Some people really do blink more when they're lying, others don't. It's about mass assumption until proven wrong and then it's only accepted when it's been proven wrong over and over again.

What you're doing when you study body language is taking multiple factors into account and making an assumption about the person that is educated and supported, but it can still be wrong. Time for another example:

The sky is blue. Water is blue. The sky has hydrogen in it. Water has hydrogen in it. The sky is loses water in the form of rain. Therefore, the sky is made of water.

The logic and the reasoning in that is sound, but it's still wrong. Something may be logical but not cogent. A person might be giving you all the logical signs that they're lying to you, but you may still be wrong. They might just be stressed or have to pee really badly. You're making an assumption that may not be cogent one hundred percent of the time.

Now, why am I telling you this? Because you need to have an open mind and be understanding that sometimes you're going to be wrong. Unfortunately for you, someone has not written a script or a book that you're a part of and you'll always be right. This is the real world, my friend, and in the real world, you're going to make mistakes.

But that's okay.

Science is about making mistakes and learning from them. Without failure, there is no progress and you're going to master the ability of actually reading people like books before you know it. But along the way, don't be worried about making some mistakes. My suggestion up front, would be keeping any accusations or assumptions you're making to yourself until they're verified. Once you get a good handle on reading those who have a secret, those lying to you, or knowing when people are distraught. Until you're a master, I'll give you some tips to give you a heads up.

Look Into My Eyes

The eyes are the windows to the soul. How many times have you heard that before? Well, with a lot of misunderstanding and some grand assumptions, a person's eyes can trick you into lying to yourself if you're not careful. The truth about the eyes is that they are a single part of a much larger picture. It's like looking at the shoulder of dear sweet Mona Lisa and that's it. You can't tell what the whole thing is if you just look at a single part. Now the face, that's a much bigger picture for you to start seeing, but it's still not the whole pie. But, it's a great place to start.

Before we get started, let's be up front about a simple fact that I think Anne Frank is going to really admire us believing in. It's the simple truth that all people are genuinely good. Even from a psychological point of view. The people that you're going to find breaking the rules most for you are going to be the people who fall into the categories of sociopaths, Machiavellians, psychopaths, pathological liars, or the mentally disturbed. These people are out there in society and they blend in for the most part, but they're going to be your most common exception to the rules. But other than that, most people are genuinely good and that means they have nothing to hide and if they do, they're probably not going to do it very well.

Humans have a whole list of microexpressions, which are involuntary nonverbal expressions that give away emotional statements. These are unavoidable and often are only repressed by the truly disturbed or paranoid. These are going to be your guides to finding out what people are conveying nonverbally.

The eyes are the most expressive part of the human body.

This is true, but they're also misread a lot. For example, a lot of people think that looking away is a sign of lying. Well, that's actually an indicator of stress. While a person may look away while you're asking them a series of questions, their eyes might convey to you that they're distressed by this line of inquiry or that they're uncomfortable, not necessarily because they're lying, but rather that they don't like this environment.

Eyes are best at expressing several things: discomfort, happiness, sadness, and anger. When someone is genuinely happy, their pleasure will manifest in their eyes with a sort of twinkling. It's easy to tell. If someone smiles at you, but their eyes do not light up, the emotion they're conveying is false. That's a safe assumption, because happiness has a clear manifestation. There is a harmony of microexpressions that add up to a person conveying happiness, even when they don't want to.

The eyes also convey discomfort in a very similar fashion. Discomfort is usually the result of stress and there are a multitude of things that cause stress in the lives of those who are talking. If you're expressing discomfort, it's usually not a clear reason that others suspect. For example, lying always comes across as discomfort because people are withholding the truth. However, discomfort also comes from thinking that you're suspected of doing something that you didn't do. Both look like lying. It's up to you to find other cues to translate these expressions into an accusation.

Sadness is impossible to fake and it take a true psychopath or someone that has fully deceived themselves to actually express a false sadness. The reason: because sadness is the devastation of a core value and if you don't have a value, you cannot fully express it in the eyes. This is often a way to find out if someone actually cared about a failure or loss that should have hurt them.

Finally, anger is another reaction that comes from an assault upon our value systems. Anger is fairly easy to fake, but usually in actions and not in expression. People get rage in their eyes and fury on their lips. It's a way to find out whether someone is actually mad or not.

If you haven't picked up already, I've mentioned how hard a lot of these expressions are to fake in the eyes and that's the key. Rather than seeing what's in the eyes, you'll be more successful in noting what isn't there. If someone should be infuriated, but their eyes translate happiness, you know they're dishonest. If they should be discomforted by what you're insinuating, but rather they stare you down, there's something wrong. It's about picking up what isn't there.

Now, let's dispel another myth about the eyes. Blinking, looking away, and touching the eyes. A lot of people believe that these are all perfect indicators that someone is lying. This is not the case. These are all indicators that someone is uncomfortable with the situation that they find themselves. In fact, people are more likely to look away when recalling an event, rather than making up an event. They look away to try and see past events. When someone refuses to break eye contact, it's usually a clear sign that they're studying you. Blinking is another habit that is constantly pointed to be an indicator of lying.

No, it's not.

When someone is blinking, know that they're uncomfortable with the situation, not that they have a subconscious tick. A small, innocent child might be blinking a lot, but not an adult when they're lying. The same goes for pupil dilation. A lot of people think that your pupils dilate when you lie. If this is the case, it's too hard to figure out on the spot. There are a myriad of variables that make this next to impossible to tell: presence of light, watery eyes from discomfort, not having a constant to measure, and just missing the constriction because you're too busy focusing on a million other microexpressions. Give up on the dilation thing, unless you're trying to play mind games and freak them out.

A place where microexpressions manifest themselves very readily is the brow. Wrinkles, crinkling, raising of an eyebrow, furrowing, or a dozen other responses escape our default veneer every time we hear something. Use this to calibrate and adjust what you're seeing in their eyes, what kind of tone your hearing and start making assumptions. Eyebrows are often features that people don't really try to master like they do their lips or eyes. When someone is mad or upset, they will furrow their brow involuntarily and usually without their awareness. Go to the bathroom now and start practicing expressions in the mirror. See how much of the expressions you perceive manifest in the brow? Now, start looking at people around you as they talk. It's a goldmine of information.

Finally, when it comes to the head. There are a lot of other things to look at. For example: women are more likely to touch their hair when they are experiencing physical attraction to. Touching of the hair usually indicates that someone is experiencing a scenario that they do not feel ready for. Whether that's dealing with an unexpected obstacle or the sudden appearance of a possible sexual partner, people touch their hair in an attempt to relieve stress.

The lips are also a host of microexpressions, and like the eyes, are a host to involuntary reactions that are rarely caught by the person talking. Very rarely can a person catch the reaction that is being broadcast in a twitch at the corners of their lips when they hear unexpected good news. It's a place to watch when you're delivering news to them that they're not expecting to hear. Another great thing is to notice the difference between a false smile and a real one. This is something you should look for in real life. They are as different as the east is from the west. Keep your eye out for them.

Now, remember how I said that looking at the eyes was kind of like looking at Mona Lisa's shoulder and trying to understand the whole picture? Well, the same is when you focus on one feature of the face. Instead, start translating expressions and note what isn't there and what is there. Read what is seen, unseen, missing, and repressed. Also, don't forget to use your ears as well. Pick up on tones and word choices that the person you're talking to is conveying. You'll begin to see whether someone is really happy for you, or secretly holding a dagger behind their back with your name on it. It's an important skill to have and you'll see that all the features work in harmony, rather than separately.

But, that's kind of like just looking at Mona and not the background. There's still so much more to read.

The Voice of Reason

Body language is not just about visual cues that you're picking up on. Nonverbal communication brings into the fold everything that you're picking up that is not an actual word, and that means how those words are spoken. It takes an incredibly fast mind to fire our deceptive or nondescript words that hide their true meaning, but masking how those words are formed is an entirely different beast to tackle.

Before we leave the face, let's spend a moment on how words are spoken. Tone, craft, emphasis, and enunciation give away more than you would ever really expect. Ever hear the phrase: "It's not what you said, but how you said it?" That is a direct contradiction to the spoken word due to the delivery of the message. So let's start with seeing how each of these four types of conversation can betray a person's true meaning.

Tone is the easiest to betray someone. When someone is trying to contradict their true emotions, they're often catching words that are flying out, repackaging them, and then letting them go on their way. The packaging is the tone. A hurt tone is nearly impossible to mask and will betray a injured or betrayed person always. The same goes with genuine anger. It's hard to mask and if the words you're hearing aren't matching the tone that they're delivered with, they're lying to you about their intention, motivation, or emotional stance in the situation.

When it comes to craft, a person lying to you is going to try and wax the poetics with what they're trying to say. Extolling you with lavished and overly flowery language is a clear indication that they're masking something and never trust someone who speaks this way as a default setting and is a well-versed socialite. There's a difference between being well-read and verbose versus a chronically deceptive two-face. Notice what words they're choosing to utilize, especially if they have a double meaning.

Emphasis is like a vortex for people who have just heard something that they're curious to know more about or want to avoid. Like a swimmer struggling to escape a whirlpool, some people will avoid topics desperately jumping from anything else that they can hide behind. Others can't avoid something that they want to know more about. Notice what it is they're clinging to and what they're desperate to avoid or know more about when they're speaking.

Finally, enunciation is another vocal tick that can give you clues as to whether someone is hiding true intentions or a personal opinion about something that they're less than honest about. It's hard to avoid speaking your mind and often a person can avoid saying negative things, but will say things in a way that emphasizes an unspoken opinion. You've experienced this before and you'll know it when you hear it. Notice when words with double meaning are emphasized or negative traits are punched at like an unguarded groin.

The lips are hard to master, but the tongue is infamously more treacherous to those trying to hide their true meanings. By seeing how thinks are spoken or what isn't spoken, you can apply this to the features of their face to get a clearer meaning of what is being said, or what isn't.

Stand Up Straight

Liars and those looking to hide something focus on their faces more than anything else. What they fail to address more often than not is the rest of their body, which is ironic, because posture and how you present yourself breathes life into everything that you're saying. Your body can contradict or emphasize everything you're saying. It's up to you to be able to translate what it is trying to broadcast to you.

While it may seem obvious that our bodies betray our thoughts, it's often something that we fail to acknowledge. Often, our own mental dissonance tends to wash out the obvious signs that something is wrong. But the poise and posture of someone can really tell you a lot about who they are or what their current mood is.

For those of you that have no clue what poise and posture is, they're basically the same thing. It's a network of physical manifestations of emotion that encompass the head, neck, shoulders, back, and hips that convey enormous amounts of information to anyone who is looking to pick up the message. It's the way you stand, the way news effects your stance physically while you receive it. It's fairly quick to pick up on and when you start to notice it, there's so much that you can actually pick up form the way a person is standing.

Let's just start with proximity. If someone is facing you as you approach, they're eager to see you, receptive. If they're standing at an angle, avoiding you, then that's exactly what they're doing. They're hoping that you'll pass up on them and keep moving. However, if their back is to you, then they really don't want you to notice them. With those basics, you can approach a conversation with huge amounts of knowledge without even having to say a word to them. But that's just the beginning.

Maybe they turn and smile at you, you already know that they're putting up a deceptive veneer to confront you with. Also, how close are they standing next to you? Do they move to approach you as you came up on them? Or did they stay put? That could also indicate how receptive they are to you or if they have private information to tell you. Closeness equates to intimacy or a stronger connection to you. The same would be if they stand farther back from you or if they do not approach you. This means that your presence is unwelcome or that they're not interested in talking with you. Read the situation before you ever start talking to help you better understand what you've gotten yourself into.

Next, let's talk about how they're standing. Are their arms folded? This is a defensive stance against you, meaning that they're not receptive to what you have to say from the start. If they start with arms crossed and lower their arms as you approach, they're letting you in. A defensive stance could be personal or it could be a reaction to the environment. It doesn't always mean that it's directed toward you. Notice their hands also. Are their fists clenched? Or are they open? This is also an indicator of tension or a lack there of.

What can be learned from a person's actual presence? Can you assume a difference between a skinny, overweight, and toned person? What's the difference between someone who is naturally skinny versus someone who has toned their body? You can tell a lot from that. Working out takes discipline, structure, dedication, a disapproval of a past self or a worrisome threat, and no small bit of vanity. An overweight body refers to other priorities and interests that extend beyond the physical. Perhaps they're just lazy? Maybe they have a condition. You won't know for certain, but again, there's a lot to be learned from what isn't there, rather than what is there.

Finally, for the overall poise and posture that they're holding, a slouch is often a clear indicator of a defeated ego or mindset. Of course, this may be habitual. They might be sloppy at standing up straight. We'll discuss the importance of incorporating habits in the next chapter, but a person who usually has decent posture but suddenly has a slouch is clearly bothered by something. The same goes for the position of their hips. A person focusing the majority of their weight onto one hip is most likely conveying a preexisting attitude or issue. This could be sarcastic, sassy, or genuine. That's up to you to determine through other indicators through the interaction, but something is up. You're approaching a mock or real danger zone. The point: it's a danger zone.

Now, noticing a person's movements are also great ways to figure out whether they're in a good attitude or not. Think about a person walking quickly and with great purpose. It's fairly obvious to picture right? Well, that's one example of how easy it is to start noticing how someone walks. A slow lethargic walk tells you more about their mindset rather than their purpose or motivation. It means that they're in no hurry to reach their destination. There might be many reasons for that, but the fact remains. They're in no hurry. Noticing the way people are walking will give you insights into how to approach their situation. If they are walking quickly and with great purpose, then you know that they're not going to be receptive to a long, drawn out conversation. Be quick and concise to keep them happy. If they're happy then you'll be able to build that rapport with them.

Noticing how someone handles their body will give you plenty of insights into how you should approach a conversation, regardless of whether you're approaching them or they're approaching you. Be sure to read the situation and keep a sense of control over the situation for everyone involved. It'll save you the effort of finding out later when they explode on you for taking too long to spit something out.

Habitual Habits

So, there are some things that we do that are not necessarily things that we broadcast for a purpose, or so we think. These are things that we've done for so long that we no longer think of them as actions, instead, they're just habits, quirks, or ticks that we've picked up along the way. Now, when you're starting out reading nonverbal signs, these might throw you for a colossal loop, making your readings wrong almost all the time. However, there's so much that can be learned from someone who has developed a habit over their lifetime.

For example, what is there to learn from a man who walks with a rigid back, shoulders squared, a limp, and a hard, observant gaze? If you were to put those pieces together, there are several things that you can pick up. The first, I would expect him to be a military man, or at the least, disciplined. Depending upon his actual build, I would say that he's most likely military. From the limp, I would assume that he's either recently hurt himself, depending upon the severity of the gait, or it's older, if the gait is softer. Depending upon his age, you can assume which war he might have served in or where he could have been stationed.

But here's where habits throw a loop. Say that man works out a lot and has a vain sense of self. Perhaps he poses in front of the mirror and likes the way he looks like an action hero when he stands and walks a certain way. The limp is from jump squats at the gym, and he struts the way he does, not out of a disciplined mindset, but out of a cocky sense of self-worth that he has carried for years.

Habits, man. They screw things up.

But let's say that you se someone who jiggles their car keys in their pockets when they're waiting in line somewhere. They do this so often that they don't even notice it or don't really consciously do it. You know what you can infer from that habit? An anxious lifestyle where time is of the extreme importance. When someone has built up a habit, it's an indicator of a lifestyle and environment that they live in.

Men who grow up in an urban environment where strutting and carrying 'swagger' around isn't an indication that they've all hurt their hips or legs? No, it shows that they want to project a sense of lethality to those around them. It's a defense mechanism. They're not soft.

People who bite their nails manifest stress through a physical tick, meaning that they have a poor coping outlet for their stress. These people are most likely high strung. The drumming of fingers means that a person is impatient and uninterested in the current usage of their time in a normal setting when this is a conscious thought, but a person who has been bored so often might develop this as a coping mechanism for any time they're alone for a second or two. This doesn't mean they're bored, it means that they've been bored a lot in the past.

Are you getting the picture right now? Actions are not always intentional, but rather indicators of a past experience. So, by making immediate assumptions about a person, based on a single interaction could steer you in the wrong direction. It's about monitoring a person and keeping track of them over a period of time to separate habits from intentional actions and then making your assumptions based on a combination of the two. Remember, habits throw off readings about the immediate situation, but they give you clear indicators to work with when it comes to past events in their life.

It's tricky, but it just takes practice.

In Perfect Harmony

The human body is a vastly complex, biological machine that is connected to an infinitely deep and sometimes contradictory nervous system that regulates and controls everything. That's why it's so impossible to control all of our microexpressions and involuntary reactions when we hear something or are having a conversation. This system and machine of flesh and blood is often hard to read, but with the right training, you'll get it down.

However, there's a saying where four blind men fall into a pit with an elephant in it with them. One grabs the trunk, the other grabs a leg, one gets a tusk, and the last guy grabs the tail. Every one of them thinks that it's something different. By looking at a single, individual part of the human body and trying to read a conversation or a person's motivations or past, is like trying to identify an elephant with just one part of it. It requires finesse and a degree of skill to step back and actually take in a person for everything that they are communicating when you are with them, near them, or spotting them across the bar.

To fully comprehend and understand the situation for the best possible results, you're going to have to work on your harmony. This is going to require a balance of monitoring what you're seeing and hearing from the person you're trying to read. Not only can you take note of their features, but you need to notice their posture, their hands, their arms, how their feet are placed, and what kind of a tone their using.

The key to harmonizing your assessment is having a strategy when approaching a person that you want to read. Start by noticing how they react with other people, if that's an option. If you see a friend near them, you'll understand what a welcomed, positive reaction is. If there's someone they're not happy with, you'll get a glimpse at what a negative reaction is. The best possible read, however, is a neutral read. If they give away nothing, you will be able to assess the situation as to whether you match the neutral control or if variables start to pop up, positive or negative.

Once you've read the person from a distance with others, take in their posture and their nonverbal attitude that hangs around them. Where are their arms? How is their posture right now? Do they have their fists clenched or are they open? Is this person standing rigid and uncomfortable or relaxed? Are they slouching in exhaustion or disappointment? Do you know that difference yet?

Next, approach them and address whatever is so important that you need to study them from afar first. What is their expression? Read their brows and their lips first. Then, read their eyes and listen carefully to how they are saying the things they're saying to you. Notice if anything changes as you talk. Do they cross their arms? Do they step away or closer? While you're standing near them, continue to assess them completely and take note of how anything might change as you continue to have this conversation with them. Build this healthy harmony so that you can pick up everything you can from them.

Harmony is a powerful tool that will help you get better reads from the person that you're studying. Remember that there is a degree of ethical restraint that you should always keep your eye on. If you're reading people to manipulate them, that's on you and it'll probably bite you in the butt if you keep trying it. But, if you're using this harmonic knowledge to get to the bottom of problems, understand others, or just to better communicate to people you know, that's great.

Your Library

To people who have studied human behavior, nonverbal communication, and body language, we're all open books to them. Of course, they're not going to be able to look at you and know that you stole that book from you elementary library when you were in the third grade, but they'll know a lot. They'll be able to work around your attitude and understand some of you secret agendas. Essentially, we all become open books in their enormous library of people who can't hide a thing from them.

If you want to be one of these people who can read all the signs, pick up on all the signals, and make the right assumptions necessary to get the information you need out of people without them ever knowing it, you've come to the right place. By implementing these practices and strategies into your daily life, you're going to be able to start understanding all the nonverbal secrets around you.

Remember that the key to mastering this skill is to keep observing people around you. The best nonverbal readers are those that constantly study people, without motive or reason, they just watch. By being a true student of observation, you'll be able to really see what makes people tick, how they work, and what is truly considered normal behavior. It's a skill that you can carry with you and you'll never be bored again. Next time you're waiting for a friend in a restaurant, checking out people at a bar, or riding the subway, you'll be able to see all the signs that are written on the faces of those around you.

But be careful, you never know who's watching you.

Conclusion

Thank you again for downloading this book!

I hope this book was able to help you to overcome the emotional neglect that you experienced as a child. Many of us believe that we will never overcome poor rearing practices until we are presented with ways to deal with the past and move towards the future. It is my hope that this book has helped you do that.

The next step in the process is to determine how you would like to progress. What are your goals in life, and how can you make these dreams your reality?

Before you go, I'd like to say thank you for purchasing my book.

I know you could have picked so many other books to read on understanding Your Emotionally Absent Mother .But you took a chance on me.

So A Big thanks for downloading this book and reading it all the way to completion.

Now I would like to ask a small favor.

Could you please take a minute or two to leave a review for this book on Amazon?

Click here

The feedback will help me continue to publish more kindle books that will help people to get better results in their lives.

And if you found it helpful in anyway then please let me know :-)

Thank you and good luck!

To your success,

Michele

Preview of My New Book..

Help! I'm In Love With A Narcissist

So There's This Person...

So you've met this person who seems to have it all together, it all figured out, and the cat's in the bag. They're the kind of person who steps into the room with the presence of a floodlight and when they leave, it feels like they took the oxygen with them. They're captivated by all the boring stuff you've crammed into your calendars and call a life, but more importantly, they make you feel great. Every word you say is scooped up and filed away in their brains because they're actively engaging with you. They're making you feel like you're the only person in the room.

I mean, they're dedicated to themselves. They've been grooming themselves impeccably, or maybe they've moved beyond that. Maybe they've transcended the need to look good and they're just all about their intellectual prowess that they're willing to share with you—YOU, mere mortal! This person is the one person you know that could sell snow to an Inuit.

Sure, they might talk like they're trying to sell you something, or you might get the chills when you shake their hand, but come on, they're really great! They're a riot to be around and there's no way that you're just going to give up on hanging out with someone this cool.

But after a while, it might grate against you. After all, you watch as they move from one person to the next at parties, dancing around like the social butterfly that they are. It might start out as jealousy that you're not getting the majority of their time. It might bother you that all that special treatment that they gave you is just their average operating mode, which they treat everyone incredible, regardless of whom they are or what their lives are like. But after a moment, the jealousy is going to fade, because there's a truth hiding in there that is just nagging at you—clawing at you—to get out.

This might be because you're picking up on something no quite right about them. It means that you might be picking up on a subtle reality that's lurking behind those charming eyes and that million dollar smile that's starting to rub you the wrong way more and more. It's something more and most likely, you're picking up on the fact that the person you're bothered by might be a narcissist.

Of course, there are Narcissists and there are narcissists. A subtle difference in writing that makes all the difference and we're going to talk about both of them in this book. There are people out there that are really full of themselves. They're people who make life difficult for themselves and for those that are working with them and there are ways for us as regular people to deal with them. There are ways around them and there are ways to truly identify them.

After all, you don't want to peg Cool Jim as a Narcissist when he just has an over inflated ego. So where do you start? Well, reading this book was a great decision, because we're going to figure out together if Cool Jim is really someone you should be avoiding or if this is someone that you should just try your hardest to ignore and maybe just avoid at parties. In the end, we're going to find out what it is that you're dealing with.

So, want to go hunting for a narcissist? Or is it a Narcissist?

O Muses

So, once upon a time, the Greeks decided that there was a story that needed to be told. It was the tale of how a river god and a nymph decided to get together for a little tryst that resulted in the birth of an exceptionally beautiful young man you was declared as Narcissus. Now, this wasn't a man who was just 90's Brad Pitt gorgeous, but the male version of Helen of Troy. He drove the ladies and the men crazy. People wanted him and they wanted to be him. There's something about this guy that really made people go wild. They wanted him and when you're a hot commodity, demand tends to turn to worship and worship does something nasty for the people who aren't ready for it.

Narcissus had a commodity that was in high demand. That means that people were all over him and the desire for him is what inevitably drove Narcissus to a dark, cold place that made him resentful and spiteful of those that loved and desired him. As they flocked to him, Narcissus became a tool and a douche. He was rude and mean and cruel to everyone that came after him. In essence, he came to believe exactly what they told him he was a little too much.

Seeing this, the goddess of revenge decided that it was time to bring him down to reality after his cruelty and rudeness toward others. So while Narcissus was out hunting all manly and such, he came across an enchanted pool that the goddess of revenge made just for him. Well, when Narcissus found the pool, he gazed into it and found his reflection and fell in love with it. For the first time in his life, Narcissus found in love with someone, only that it's himself. Gazing into the pool, night and day passed as he gazed at the reflection in the pool.

Then, before anyone can tell him what an idiot he's being, his selfish love is rewarded with him falling into the pool and drowning because he couldn't take his eyes off himself.

There's a lot that can be taken away from this story and there's a lot that is freakishly familiar with what's going to follow in these next few chapters. So there's this happy little moment at the end of this chapter that I get to tell you why this story is important and it's going to be great. So here you go:

Click Here To Read The Rest Of
Help! I'm In Love With A Narcissist

P.S. You'll find many more books like this and others under my name Michele Gilbert.

Don't miss them... here is a short list.

Wicca: The Ultimate Beginners Guide For Witches and Warlocks: Learn Wicca Magic

The Introvert's Advantage: The Introverts Guide To Succeeding In An Extrovert World

Stop Playing Mind Games: How To Free Yourself Of Controlling And Manipulating Relationships

Instant Charisma: A Quick And Easy Guide To Talk, Impress, And Make Anyone Like You

Chakras: Understanding The 7 Main Chakras For Beginners: The Ultimate Guide To Chakra Mindfulness, Balance and Healing

Practicing Mindfulness: Living in the moment through Meditation: Everyday Habits and Rituals to help you achieve inner peace

Adrenal Fatigue: What Is Adrenal Fatigue Syndrome And How To Reset Your Diet And Your Life

Sleep Tight: Overcome Insomnia and Sleep Disorders for a better more restful sleep!

Stop Back Pain Now!: Back Pain Remedies and Treatments so you can live a pain free life!

The Arthritis Pain Cure: How to find Arthritis Pain Relief and live a happy pain free life!

The Headache Pain Cure: How to find Headache Pain Relief and live a happy Pain Free Life!

Stop Panic Attacks and Anxiety Disorders without Drugs Now!: Overcome Panic, Stress and Anxiety and live a happy pain free life!

The Breakup Recovery Guide: Advice for Surviving Heartbreak, Letting Go and Thriving in an exciting new life!

The Friendship Guide to Finding Friends Forever: How to Find, Make and Keep Quality Friendships After your Breakup

The Credit Fix: Leave behind credit card debt and poor credit scores and get your life back!

How To Stop Being Jealous And Insecure: Overcome Insecurity And Relationship Jealousy

So I Am Dating A Psycopath: Now What?

Michele Gilbert was born and raised in Brooklyn, New York. Drawn to literature and writing at a young age, she enrolled at Brooklyn College and majored in English. After graduation Michele did not begin writing immediately, instead she embarked on a career in the finance industry and spent the next thirty years on Wall Street.

Serendipity struck when she least expected it. After ending a long-term relationship, Michele found herself lost and unsure what the future held. She began to read books on grief and loss, looking for answers. Those led her to delve deeper into the Law of Attraction and its power. What resulted was remarkable. Not only had she begun to heal, she had also rekindled her former love of writing and discovered her life's purpose.

The years have taken her through many twists and turns, but she learned valuable lessons along the way. Today she publishes books-mostly self-help and metaphysical in nature-and feels compelled to share her knowledge with those facing similar experiences. Her greatest hope is to inspire others and show them ways to overcome adversity and gracefully accept life's inevitable low points.

Going forward, she plans to incorporate more teachings of self-help, finance and meditation. Regular meditation is very beneficial to her progress as she forges a new life. Morning rituals and positive incantations are other practices Michele embraces; they are very restorative in daily life.

As an avid hiker, Michele and fellow club members often hike the picturesque Jersey Pine Barrens. She is a history buff, voracious reader, baseball fanatic and a foodie. She also proudly supports Trout Unlimited-a national non-profit organization dedicated to conserving, protecting and restoring North America's Coldwater fisheries and their watersheds.

Michele currently resides forty minutes from Atlantic City and the Jersey Shore. She makes her home with a Blue Russian rescue cat named Jersey, though she isn't exactly sure who rescued who.

Michele really enjoys publishing books that can make a difference in people's lives. If you have any suggestions or would like to have a specific topic covered in a future book, please send an email to michelegilbertbooks@gmail.com and we will get back to you.

Thanks for reading!

www.ingramcontent.com/pod-product-compliance
Lightning Source LLC
Chambersburg PA
CBHW050927290526
45792CB00002B/912